COLLECTION EDITOR: **JENNIFER GRÜNWALD**
ASSOCIATE MANAGING EDITOR: **KATERI WOODY**
ASSOCIATE EDITOR: **SARAH BRUNSTAD**
EDITOR, SPECIAL PROJECTS: **MARK D. BEAZLEY**
VP, PRODUCTION & SPECIAL PROJECTS: **JEFF YOUNGQUIST**
SVP PRINT, SALES & MARKETING: **DAVID GABRIEL**
BOOK DESIGNER: **ADAM DEL RE**

EDITOR IN CHIEF: **AXEL ALONSO**
CHIEF CREATIVE OFFICER: **JOE QUESADA**
PUBLISHER: **DAN BUCKLEY**
EXECUTIVE PRODUCER: **ALAN FINE**

THOR CREATED BY **STAN LEE**, **LARRY LIEBER** & **JACK KIRBY**

MIGHTY THOR VOL. 2: LORDS OF MIDGARD. Contains material originally published in magazine form as MIGHTY THOR #6-12. First printing 2016. ISBN# 978-0-7851-9523-8. Published by MARV WORLDWIDE, INC., a subsidiary of MARVEL ENTERTAINMENT, LLC. OFFICE OF PUBLICATION: 135 West 50th Street, New York, NY 10020. Copyright © 2016 MARVEL No similarity between any of names, characters, persons, and/or institutions in this magazine with those of any living or dead person or institution is intended, and any such similarity which may exist is purely coincidental. **Print in the U.S.A.** ALAN FINE, President, Marvel Entertainment; DAN BUCKLEY, President, TV, Publishing & Brand Management; JOE QUESADA, Chief Creative Officer; TOM BREVOORT, SVP of Publishi DAVID BOGART, SVP of Business Affairs & Operations, Publishing & Partnership; C.B. CEBULSKI, VP of Brand Management & Development, Asia; DAVID GABRIEL, SVP of Sales & Marketing, Publishi JEFF YOUNGQUIST, VP of Production & Special Projects; DAN CARR, Executive Director of Publishing Technology; ALEX MORALES, Director of Publishing Operations; SUSAN CRESPI, Production Manag STAN LEE, Chairman Emeritus. For information regarding advertising in Marvel Comics or on Marvel.com, please contact Vit DeBellis, Integrated Sales Manager, at vdebellis@marvel.com. For Mar subscription inquiries, please call 888-511-5480. **Manufactured between 9/16/2016 and 10/31/2016 by LSC COMMUNICATIONS INC., SALEM, VA, USA.**

10 9 8 7 6 5 4 3 2 1

THE MIGHTY THOR

LORDS OF MIDGARD

WRITER	ARTIST	COLOR ARTIST
ASON AARON	**RUSSELL DAUTERMAN**	**MATTHEW WILSON**

ART & COLOR, #6-7 VIKING ERA	ART & COLOR, #12 OLD ASGARD
RAFA GARRES	**FRAZER IRVING**

LETTERER	COVER ART
VC's JOE SABINO	**RUSSELL DAUTERMAN & MATTHEW WILSON**

ASSISTANT EDITORS	EDITOR
CHRIS ROBINSON & CHARLES BEACHAM	**WIL MOSS**

WHEN **DR. JANE FOSTER** LIFTS THE MYSTIC HAMMER MJOLNIR, SHE IS
TRANSFORMED INTO **THE GODDESS OF THUNDER, THE MIGHTY THOR!**
HER ENEMIES ARE MANY, AS ASGARD DESCENDS FURTHER INTO CHAOS
AND WAR THREATENS TO SPREAD THROUGHOUT THE TEN REALMS.
YET HER GREATEST BATTLE WILL BE AGAINST A FAR MORE PERSONAL FOE:
THE CANCER THAT IS KILLING HER MORTAL FORM...

DESPITE THOR'S SEEMINGLY DECISIVE DEFEAT OF MALEKITH'S FORCES,
THE KING OF THE DARK ELVES CONVINCED THE ENCHANTRESS
TO CAST A SPELL OF COERCION OVER AELSA, QUEEN OF THE LIGHT ELVES.
UNDER THIS ENCHANTEMENT, AELSA MARRIED MALEKITH,
GIVING THE MONSTER CONTROL OF ALFHEIM. A BEAUTIFUL REALM RICH
WITH RESOURCES, ALFHEIM IS NOW SUBJECT TO THE WILL AND WHIM
OF THE DARK ELF KING AND HIS GREEDY ALLIES...

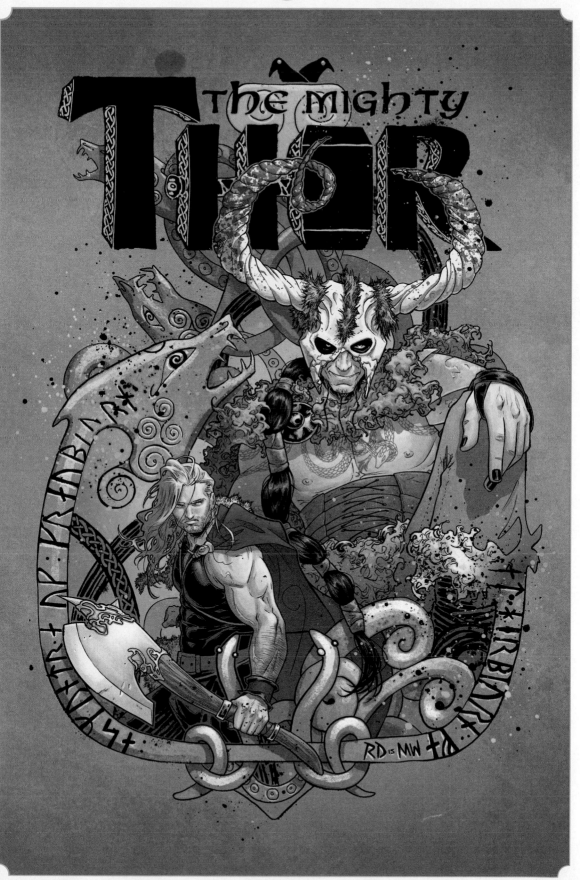

6

THE STRONGEST VIKING THERE IS PART I

MY ALLIANCE WITH MALEKITH HAS ALREADY PROVEN QUITE FRUITFUL.

ROXXON NOW MINES FOR COAL IN THE SWAMPS OF SVARTALFHEIM AND DRILLS FOR OIL HERE ON THE PLANES OF ALFHEIM, WITH OTHER RESOURCES AND REALMS SURE TO FOLLOW.

ONCE OUR TRANS-REALM PIPELINE IS ESTABLISHED, WE WILL BE MAKING BILLIONS PER DAY OFF THIS ARRANGEMENT.

AND YET...

DARIO AGGER. C.E.O. OF ROXXON ENERGY CORPORATION. ALSO SOMETIMES A MINOTAUR.

...YET I AM INCREASINGLY AWARE OF THE FACT THAT I AM IN LEAGUE WITH *SORCERERS* AND *GIANTS*.

THE ROXXON ARMORIES HOLD ENOUGH WEAPONS TO ANNIHILATE ANY ARMY ON EARTH. BUT WE'RE NOT DEALING WITH THINGS OF THE *EARTH* ANYMORE, ARE WE?

IF MALEKITH SHOULD EVER DECIDE TO ALTER OUR AGREEMENT...

YOU ARE OUTGUNNED. YOU NEED WEAPONS.

I NEED *ALLIES* AGAINST MY *ALLIES*. AND SOMETHING TELLS ME...

...YOU DO, TOO. OR HAS YOUR FATHER LAUFEY SUDDENLY DECIDED *NOT* TO MURDER YOU?

WELL, HE HASN'T TRIED TOO MANY TIMES *TODAY.* SO THERE'S ALWAYS HOPE, I SUPPOSE.

LOKI. GOD OF LIES, PRINCE OF JOTUNHEIM.

BUT ONE CAN NEVER HAVE TOO MANY FRIENDS IN A TIME OF WAR, I ALWAYS SAY. WHAT WOULD YOU ASK OF ME, FRIEND?

MALEKITH HAS HIS WAR WITCHES AND BAT RIDERS. HIS ARMY OF ELVES HAS ONLY GROWN SINCE CONQUERING ALFHEIM.

AND NOW I HEAR RUMORS OF SOME NEW MONSTER OF HIS, SOMETHING CALLED *KURSE.*

I NEED TO BALANCE THE SCALES. I NEED MORE MONSTERS OF MY OWN.

AH, I SEE. WELL THEN YOU'VE COME TO THE RIGHT PLACE, DARIO AGGER.

I'VE MADE JUST THESE SORTS OF DEALS BEFORE.

ALLOW ME, IF YOU WILL, TO TELL YOU A STORY.

ONE THAT BEGINS, LONG AGO...

"...IN THE AGE OF *THE VIKINGS.*

MIDGARD.
SHORES OF THE
SKAGERRAK.
896 A.D.

"*BODOLF THE BLACK* WAS A FEARSOME YOUNG CHIEFTAIN WITH AN UNQUENCHABLE THIRST FOR COMBAT AND GLORY. IT WAS SAID THAT HE AND HIS BERSERKERS HAD NEVER LOST A BATTLE.

"BODOLF'S SECRET WAS THAT HE SAID A PRAYER TO *THE GOD OF THUNDER* BEFORE EACH FIGHT. AND HIS PRAYERS WERE ALWAYS ANSWERED.

KRAKA-TOOOM

"SOMETIMES IN WAYS HE NEVER IMAGINED."

COME, YOU DOGS!

THROUGH THOR LIES THE WAY TO VALHALLA!

HA HA HA!

"BODOLF THE BLACK FOUND RIVALS BOTH ABROAD AND AT HOME. AND FELLED THEM ALL.

"BODOLF'S FAME GREW QUICKLY. AS DID HIS WEALTH."

HAIL TO BODOLF!

"AND HIS GREED."

HAIL TO BODOLF *THE UNSTOPPABLE!* NONE DARE OPPOSE US!

IF NONE DARE, THEN WE SHALL DARE FOR THEM.

HA. JUST DON'T FORGET TO SAY YOUR PRAYERS, BODOLF.

I WILL CONTINUE TO AID YOU. ≠HIC≠

"BUT NOTHING GREW MORE QUICKLY THAN HIS *PRIDE*."

THE DAY IS OURS! ANOTHER LEGENDARY VICTORY FOR BODOLF THE BLACK!

HEH.

FOR *THOR*, YOU MEAN.

WHAT WOULD *MIGHTY BODOLF* BE WITHOUT HIS *PET GOD* BY HIS SIDE? HUH?

NOTHING, THAT'S-- NNNRGH!

"WITH EACH BATTLE WON, BODOLF BEGAN TO FIND HIMSELF MORE RELUCTANT THAN EVER TO BEND HIS KNEE.

"EVEN TO THE GODS.

"ESPECIALLY TO THE GODS.

"BODOLF LEARNED THE SAME LESSON ALL THE OTHER FOOLS HAD.

"MEN ARE MEN AND GODS ARE GODS. AND THIS...

"THIS IS WHY THE ONE PRAYS TO THE OTHER.

"BODOLF'S ARMY WAS ROUTED. HIS LANDS WERE SEIZED. HIS WEALTH WAS PILLAGED. HIS WIVES ABANDONED HIM.

"BODOLF THE BLACK, SCOURGE OF THE SKAGERRAK, WAS NOW BODOLF THE *BROKEN*. BODOLF THE *DESTITUTE*.

"BODOLF KNEW RIGHT AWAY WHERE HE'D GONE WRONG, AND WHAT HE HAD TO DO TO SET THINGS RIGHT.

"BODOLF *PRAYED*.

"JUST AS HE HAD ONCE PRAYED BEFORE EVERY BATTLE.

"ONLY THIS TIME, THE WORDS WERE DIFFERENT.

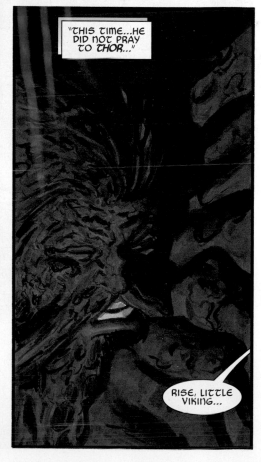

"THIS TIME...HE DID NOT PRAY TO *THOR*..."

RISE, LITTLE VIKING...

THE POWER TO BATTLE MY BROTHER. TO LAY HIM LOW. "TO BREAK HIS BASTARD BONES," I BELIEVE YOU SAID.

AYE. I DID.

I LIKE YOU ALREADY, BODOLF THE BOLD. THOUGH SUCH A MIGHTY BOON IS NOT SO EASILY GRANTED.

FOR THE STRENGTH OF A GOD DOES NOT BELONG IN A MORTAL FORM. MANY MEN HAVE TRIED, BUT FEW COULD EVER CONTAIN SUCH POWER FOR LONG.

ARE YOU SURE YOU ARE PREPARED FOR SUCH A CHALLENGE?

IF NOT, MAY DOGS EAT MY CHILDREN. MAY HELA FEED ME FOR ALL ETERNITY TO THE SPIDERS OF HEL.

HEH. DISAPPOINT ME, LITTLE VIKING, AND I ASSURE YOU, DOGS AND SPIDERS WILL BE THE LEAST OF YOUR WORRIES.

NOW DO EXACTLY AS I SAY...

FIRST, YOU'RE GOING TO NEED A BOAT.

"THEY BATTLED FOR THREE DAYS AND THREE NIGHTS.

"THE DRAGON'S HEART WAS SO HOT, IT MELTED HIS BLADE.

"SO BODOLF TORE ITS GUTS OUT WITH HIS OWN FLAMING HANDS.

"AND THEN HE SAID THE WORDS THAT LOKI HAD TOLD HIM TO SAY.

"AND DRANK THE DRAGON'S BLOOD UNTIL HE VOMITED FIRE.

"AND THEN THE *REAL* PAIN BEGAN."

RAAAAGH!!!

"ALL HE COULD REMEMBER OF THE NEXT FEW DAYS WAS HIS OWN SCREAMING. BUT LOKI ASSURED HIM HE WAS READY."

THOR!

BODOLF APPROACHES!

"SO BODOLF SENT FORTH A CHALLENGE. ONE THAT WAS EAGERLY ANSWERED."

HA! BODOLF! YOU SEEM TO HAVE FORGOTTEN YOUR ARMY.

THIS IS MADNESS. HE PLANS TO FIGHT US ALONE? HE DOESN'T EVEN HAVE A SWORD.

NOW THIS, THIS IS A VIKING! WELL DONE, BODOLF! WHAT A TALE YOU WILL TAKE WITH YOU TO VALHALLA!

WHAT I WILL TAKE... ARE YOUR HEADS.

AND THEN YOUR HOMES. AND THEN YOUR WOMEN.

AND NO GOD IN THE HEAVENS CAN SAVE YOU.

≠P-TEW≠ MADNESS OR NOT, I SAY WE KILL HIM.

AYE.

DEATH TO BODOLF!

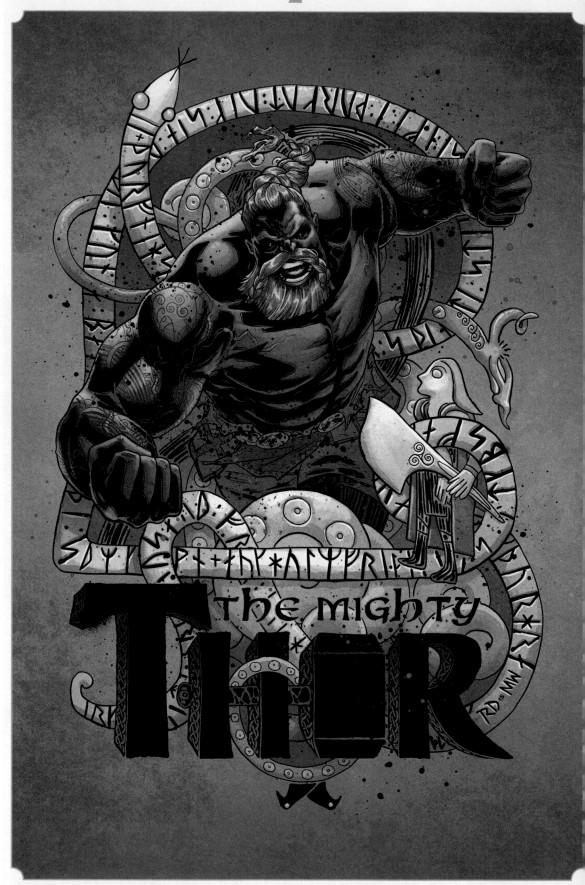

7

THE MIGHTY THOR

THE STRONGEST VIKING THERE IS PART II

ASGARD.
IN THE AGE OF
THE VIKINGS.

"ALL THANKS TO ME, OF COURSE.

"LOKI, BUILDER OF MEN. FULFILLER OF DREAMS.

"SUDDENLY, MY TALLY OF INCOMING PRAYERS BEGAN TO SKYROCKET. IT WAS A VERY GOOD SUMMER.

"UNLESS YOU HAPPENED TO DRAW THE IRE OF BODOLF THE BLACK. WHICH MANY DID.

"THOUGH USUALLY NOT FOR LONG.

"BODOLF AND HIS GROWING ARMY CONQUERED AND PILLAGED AT WILL.

"IT WAS SAID THAT NONE COULD OPPOSE HIM.

"ON MIDGARD...

"...OR ANY OTHER REALM."

I SEE ANOTHER VICTORY FOR BODOLF THE...

TO HEL WITH MIDGARD.

IF ANYONE PRAYS TO ME, TELL THEM I'M BUSY...BUSY BEING...

BLAURRRGGHH!

"BODOLF WAS THE STRONGEST VIKING WARLORD IN ALL THE LAND.

"HE HAD EVERYTHING HE'D EVER WANTED. WOMEN. WEALTH. MORE POWER THAN HE COULD IMAGINE.

"BUT HUMANS ARE THE SIMPLEST OF FOOLS. CONTENTMENT IS SIMPLY NOT IN THEIR NATURE.

"NO MATTER HOW OFTEN YOU SATE THEIR HUNGER...

"...THEY ALWAYS FIND NEW WAYS IN WHICH TO STARVE."

STOP. LAUGHING.

...IT WILL NOT SAVE YOU FROM HELA'S DARK EMBRA--

I KNOW NOT WHAT DARK MAGIC YOU HAVE CONJURED TO DEFORM YOURSELF SO, BUT I SWEAR TO YOU, BODOLF...

WHUGH!

"THE GROUND QUAKED FOR MILES. THE SEAS SWELLED AND CRASHED. THUNDER SHOOK THE SKIES ALL OVER THE WORLD.

"SUCH A DISPLAY OF POWER... DID NOT GO UNNOTICED, AS I WOULD EVENTUALLY LEARN ALL TOO WELL."

COME AWAY, PRINCESS. THESE BEASTS ARE OF THE SURFACE. THEIR RUTTING IS NO CONCERN OF THE FUTURE QUEEN OF ATLANTIS.

YES, OF COURSE.

BUT... SOMEDAY...

KRAKA-THOOOM

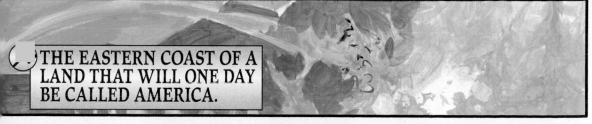

THE EASTERN COAST OF A LAND THAT WILL ONE DAY BE CALLED AMERICA.

I SMELL IT TOO, GIRL.

THERE IS VENGEANCE IN THE AIR. BUT THIS IS NOT OUR FIGHT.

NOT YET.

"IN THE MYSTICAL CITY OF K'UN-LUN, *SHOU-LAO THE DRAGON* WAS DISTRACTED BY THE RUMBLE OF DISTANT THUNDER, LONG ENOUGH FOR A FIST TO PLUNGE DEEP INTO ITS HEART.

"IN THE GREAT NORTHERN WILDS, A GIANT SHAGGY *BEAST* HOWLED AT THE SKY.

"ON THE PLAINS OF AFRICA, A *PANTHER* SNARLED.

"BUT THOSE ARE STORIES FOR ANOTHER DAY, PERHAPS."

WHAT IN THE NAME OF ODIN...?!

RRRRRRRRGGGHHHH!!!

LORD THOR?

HARDER, YOU MORONIC BEAST!

SMASH HIS PRETTY LITTLE FACE. MAKE HIM KNOW HOW IT FEELS TO BE *BROKEN*. TO LOOK IN THE MIRROR AND SEE ONLY UGLINESS.

DO IT! BEAT HIM INTO A SACK OF BLOND MUSH!

"WHILE I WAS BUSY REPRIMANDING MY OWN REBELLIOUS CREATION-- UNFORTUNATELY AN ALL-TOO-FAMILIAR THEME FOR ME--THE GOD OF THUNDER WAS CATCHING HIS SECOND WIND."

"AS ONLY THE GOD OF THUNDER CAN."

NOW... WHERE WERE WE?

PERHAPS... I'VE DONE MY WORK TOO WELL.

BODOLF FEARS NO GOD!

BODOLF IS THE STRONGEST ON ALL OF MIDGARD!

NO, BODOLF...

...NOT THIS DAY.

UNH!

MOMENTS LATER, ON THE OTHER SIDE OF THE GLOBE.

THOR!

YOU CAN'T WAIT TO TELL FATHER OF THIS, CAN YOU?

TELL HIM WHAT? THAT A LYING, HATEFUL DEVIL LIVES IN HIS MIDST?

THIS THE ALL-FATHER KNOWS.

STILL...IT IS TIME TO COME HOME, BROTHER. AND TIME TO END THIS FARCE OF A--

OH, SPARE ME YOUR LECTURES, "BROTHER"! I'VE HEARD THEM ALL!

THE THRONE OF ASGARD WILL SUIT YOU WELL SOMEDAY, LITTLE LORD OF SANCTIMONY!

MARK MY WORDS THAT WHENEVER THAT DAY COMES...

...WHEN ALL YOUR DREAMS LIE BEFORE YOU IN GLEAMING, GOLDEN SPLENDOR...

...LOKI WILL BE THERE TO MAKE THEM ALL BURN.

UNTIL THAT DAY THEN, BROTHER.

UNTIL THAT DAY.

"AND SO WE REACH THE END OF MY TALE, THOUGH IN TRUTH, STORIES NEVER TRULY END, DO THEY? ONE MERELY BLEEDS INTO THE NEXT."

"SO THE SAGA OF THE EPIC BATTLE BETWEEN THOR AND BODOLF THE BLACK...BECOMES THE STORY OF A LONELY VIKING, WANDERING THE EARTH, FIGHTING TO SUPPRESS THE MONSTER INSIDE HIM."

HRRRGGHH!!!

THAT'S... HIGHER THAN THE LAST TIME.

"AND THE STORY OF A GOD STILL STRIVING TO BE WORTHY."

"AND OF A LOKI WHO WOULD SOMEDAY...

"WELL...SOME STORIES ARE STILL YET TO BE WRITTEN."

"...WE'LL TALK ABOUT WHAT YOU OWE ME."

JUST... JUST NAME YOUR PRICE.

I WANT A CHURCH.

A BIG ONE.

I MISS THE PRAYER.

GODS, DO I MISS THE PRAYER.

STORIES NEVER END.

ONLY LIVES AND WORLDS DO THAT.

STORIES, WE JUST KEEP ON TELLING.

FOR AS LONG AS THERE'S ANYONE FOOLISH ENOUGH TO LISTEN.

8

LORDS OF MIDGARD

SEBASTIAN SHAW,
PRINCIPAL OWNER,
SHAW INDUSTRIES.

DARREN CROSS,
FOUNDER,
CROSS TECHNOLOGICAL
ENTERPRISES.

MEETINGS HAVE BEEN TAKING PLACE AT THIS TABLE FOR MANY YEARS. LONG BEFORE MOST OF US WERE BORN.

THESE MEETINGS...DON'T HAVE A NAME. NO RECORD OF THEM HAS EVER EXISTED OR EVER WILL.

THERE ARE THOSE OUTSIDE THIS ROOM WHO WOULD LABEL WHAT HAPPENS HERE AS COLLUSION.

OF COURSE, WE PREFER TO THINK OF THESE PROCEEDINGS AS MERELY... PROFESSIONAL COURTESIES.

EZEKIEL STANE,
CEO, STANE INTERNATIONAL.

SHINGEN HARADA,
CEO, THE YASHIDA CORPORATION.

FRR'DOX,
SUPREME DIRECTOR OF
INTERSTELLAR OPERATIONS,
SHI'AR SOLUTIONS CONSOLIDATED.

WILHELMINA
KENSINGTON,
ACTING CEO, KILGORE ARMS.

THERE ARE NO FRIENDS OR ALLIES IN THIS ROOM. ONLY PEERS.

AS CONFIRMED BY THE CONTENTS OF OUR BANK ACCOUNTS. PEERS AND PROFESSIONAL COURTESIES.

WILSON FISK,
PRESIDENT, FISK INDUSTRIES.

UNFORTUNATELY, WE ARE CALLED HERE TODAY BECAUSE ONE AMONG US HAS OF LATE BEEN RATHER DISAPPOINTINGLY...

...DISCOURTEOUS.

"SO...WHAT'S THIS...UM... ABOUT THOR?"

S.H.I.E.L.D. DOESN'T BELIEVE IN SECRET IDENTITIES, MS. FOSTER.

S.H.I.E.L.D. DOESN'T LIKE IT WHEN SOMEONE KEEPS SECRETS FROM US.

ESPECIALLY WHEN THAT SOMEONE IS ONE OF THE MOST POWERFUL BEINGS ON THE PLANET.

THOSE KINDS OF PEOPLE AREN'T ENTITLED TO SECRETS.

WE NEED TO KNOW WHO THEY ARE AND IF WE CAN TRUST THEM.

OR IF WE CAN'T TRUST THEM.

S.H.I.E.L.D. HAS AN ENTIRE DIVISION DEVOTED TO UNCOVERING SECRET IDENTITIES.

AND WE'RE IT.

WE KNEW TONY STARK WAS IRON MAN BEFORE HIS GIRLFRIEND DID.

WE KNEW SHE-HULK WAS SOME TWO-BIT LAWYER.

WE KNEW DOCTOR STRANGE WAS...DOCTOR STRANGE.

AND WE KNEW THAT THE OLD THOR, THE BEARDED THOR...ONCE PRETENDED TO BE A DOCTOR CALLED DONALD BLAKE.

DONALD BLAKE. YOUR FORMER BOSS.

YOUR FORMER BOYFRIEND.

NOT REALLY.

YOU SEE WHERE THIS IS GOING, MS. FOSTER?

NOW THERE'S A *NEW* THOR RUNNING AROUND.

HAS A *MASK* ON HER HELMET.

ONLY ONE REASON SOMEONE WEARS A MASK.

MEANS THEY'VE GOT SOMETHING TO *HIDE*.

YOU KNEW THE OLD THOR WELL, DIDN'T YOU, MS. FOSTER?

EVEN KNEW HIM IN THE *BIBLICAL* SENSE.

NOW YOU LIVE ON ASGARD.

ASGARDIA.

WHATEVER.

SOMETHING TELLS ME, MS. FOSTER...THAT YOU KNOW MORE ABOUT THIS NEW THOR THAN YOU'RE TELLING US.

YOU KNOW WHO SHE *IS*, DON'T YOU?

WE'RE S.H.I.E.L.D. IF YOU DECIDE TO PLAY HARDBALL WITH US, WE CAN MAKE YOUR LIFE VERY DIFFICULT.

VERY, *VERY* DIFFICULT.

TELL US WHAT YOU KNOW, MS. FOSTER.

TELL US THOR'S SECRET IDENTITY.

OR *ELSE*.

OR A VERY *BIG* ELSE.

HA HA HA HAAA HA!

DID I MISS A *JOKE*?

THIS IS S.H.I.E.L.D. NO JOKES ARE ALLOWED.

I'M DYING OF *CANCER*, YOU JACKASSES.

WHAT EXACTLY DO YOU THINK YOU'VE GOT THAT YOU CAN *THREATEN* ME WITH?

WOULD YOU LIKE ME TO MAKE A LIST?

WHAT THE HELL IS THIS?

BECAUSE I KNOW IT CAN'T BE WHAT IT LOOKS LIKE.

BECAUSE WHAT IT LOOKS LIKE IS TWO GROWN JERKWADS TRYING TO INTIMIDATE A VERY SICK WOMAN.

MIND YOUR OWN BUSINESS, *AGENT SOLOMON.*

MY APOLOGIES ON BEHALF OF S.H.I.E.L.D., MA'AM. YOU CAN GO NOW.

NO, YOU CAN'T.

NO, SHE CAN'T.

I'D BE HAPPY TO GIVE YOU A LIFT BACK TO THE CITY.

THIS ISN'T OVER.

FOR YOUR SAKES, IT HAD BETTER BE.

MS. FOSTER, I WOULDN'T RECOMMEND YOU WALK OUT THAT--

IT'S *DR. FOSTER,* ACTUALLY. AND NEXT TIME YOU HAVE QUESTIONS FOR ME, YOU CAN CALL MY LAWYER.

YOU'LL LIKE HER. SHE'S BIG AND GREEN AND LOVES TO SMASH THINGS.

GOOD DAY, AGENTS.

I'M REALLY SORRY, DR. FOSTER, BUT I'M AFRAID I'M GONNA HAVE TO...

PLEASE, ROZ, CALL ME JANE.

AND AFTER YOU'RE DONE KICKING ROXXON'S ASS...I EXPECT A CALL ABOUT THAT COFFEE.

ALFHEIM, WHERE MALEKITH HAS BEWITCHED THE QUEEN. JOTUNHEIM, WHERE LOKI HIDES BEHIND HIS FROST GIANT FATHER.

AVENGERS HEADQUARTERS IN JERSEY. WHEREVER THE HELL THE OTHER THOR HAS DISAPPEARED TO.

THERE ARE A MILLION DIFFERENT PLACES I SHOULD BE RIGHT NOW.

ASGARDIA, WHERE A SERPENT SITS ON THE THRONE AND THE CONGRESS OF WORLDS IS IN CHAOS. SWITZERLAND, WHERE ROXXON IS APPARENTLY BEING ROXXON AGAIN.

AND NONE OF THEM ARE HERE.

McCARTHY MEDICAL INSTITUT

MARIA WHEELOCK CANCER CENT

YEAH, YEAH, I KNOW, STOP LOOKING AT ME LIKE THAT.

ME TRYING NOT TO DIE WILL HAVE TO WAIT UNTIL TOMORROW. RIGHT NOW THE EARTH DOESN'T NEED A SICKLY DOCTOR FROM STATEN ISLAND.

IT NEEDS THE GODDESS OF THUNDER.

AND I NEED DIRECTIONS TO SWITZERLAND. DOES THIS HAMMER HAVE GPS?

BOSS JUST TRIGGERED HIS WATCH ALARM. THIS IS A PRIORITY-ONE ALERT.

ALL ROXXON AGENTS, GET IN THERE!

COPY THAT.

AH, SO GOOD TO SEE YOU AGAIN, MA'AM. HOW MAY WE HELP YOU TODAY?

I BELIEVE THIS SHOULD COVER IT.

AH, I'M SORRY, BUT COVER WHAT?

THE DAMAGES.

YOU COME AT ME...WITH A FANCY SUIT OF ARMOR AND A SWORD?

YOU HAVE NO IDEA WHAT YOU'RE DEALING WITH, BOY!

RRGGH?

fwhip

WHAT *YOU'RE* NOW DEALING WITH, DARIO AGGER, IS ROUGHLY 20,000 VOLTS.

HHHRRRRRGGGHH!

I JUST MISSED IT, COULSON.

BUT SOMETHING DEFINITELY HAPPENED HERE. THE LOBBY'S FILLED WITH DEAD ROXXON SECURITY AGENTS.

THINK I MIGHT NEED *BACKUP* ON THIS ONE.

COULSON. BELAY THAT REQUEST.

I THINK MY BACKUP JUST ARRIVED.

DARIO AGGER OF *ROXXON!*

PREPARE TO ANSWER FOR YOUR CRIMES, YOU FOUL BEAST!

9

THE AGGER IMPERATIVE

THEY WERE GOING TO **KILL** YOU.

MALEKITH. THAT WAS HIS PLAN ALL ALONG.

YOU AS THE ALL-MOTHER... **FRIGHTENED** HIM.

HE WANTS A **BORSON** ON THE THRONE OF ASGARD. WHETHER THAT'S **ODIN** OR HIS BROTHER **CUL**, MALEKITH DOESN'T CARE.

ONE IS JUST AS GOOD AS THE OTHER WHEN IT COMES TO BEING HEADSTRONG AND STUBBORN AND WILLFULLY BLIND TO THE PLIGHT OF THE OTHER REALMS.

MY LORD.

YOU CANNOT KEEP DOING THIS DAY AFTER DAY. EVEN ONE OF YOUR OMNIPOTENCE WILL SURELY...

LET HER DRINK.

EVERY LAST DROP, IF THAT'S WHAT IT TAKES.

ASGARD WILL STAY OUT OF THE WAR OF REALMS. UNTIL IT'S TOO LATE.

MALEKITH WAS GOING TO ENSURE THAT, ONE WAY OR THE OTHER.

THAT'S WHY I HAD TO ACT, MOTHER. THAT'S WHY I HAD TO BE THE ONE TO...

...TO SAVE YOU.

I SWEAR, JUST THIS ONCE...

I'M NOT LYING.

THOUGH FOR THAT TO BE TRUE...IT MEANS YOU CANNOT DIE, LADY FREYJA.

PLEASE DON'T DIE, MOTHER. PLEASE DON'T...

I FAIL TO UNDERSTAND, AGENT SOLOMON. YOU SAID WE WOULD BE RUSHING HEADLONG INTO GREAT DANGER.

YEAH, WELL, WE ARE, BELIEVE ME, THOR. IT'S...UH...AROUND HERE *SOMEWHERE.*

YOU'LL KNOW IT WHEN YOU SEE IT.

I HAVE THE EYES OF A GODDESS, BUT I SEE NAUGHT BUT ICE AND EMPTY OCEAN. WHY HAVE WE COME TO THIS PLACE?

AND WHAT DOES THIS HAVE TO DO WITH *DARIO AGGER* OF ROXXON?

EVERYTHING.

A FEW MONTHS AGO I WAS APPROACHED BY A DISGRUNTLED ROXXON PROGRAMMER. HE WAS THINKING OF BREAKING HIS N.D.A. AND SPILLING THE BEANS ON HIS EMPLOYERS.

HE WOULDN'T TELL ME MUCH, BUT HE DID KEEP MENTIONING SOMETHING CALLED *ICE STATION PRIME.*

COMMENCING ADVANCED RADAR SCAN.

ROXXON'S MAIN COMPUTER HUB. HIDDEN SOMEWHERE IN THE SOUTHERN OCEAN. HE NEVER GAVE ME THE EXACT COORDINATES, THOUGH.

AND TWO DAYS AFTER I MET HIM, THE BRAKES AND SEATBELT ON HIS ROXX-AM SPORTS CAR MYSTERIOUSLY FAILED AND HE WAS DEAD.

WE FIND THAT COMPUTER HUB, IT JUST MIGHT GIVE US THE EVIDENCE WE NEED TO FINALLY BRING ROXXON CRUMBLING DOWN.

TO MAKE THEM PAY FOR WHAT THEY'VE DONE TO THIS PLANET. AND ALL THE PEOPLE THEY'VE CRUSHED ALONG THE WAY.

FOR WHAT THEY DID TO *BROXTON, OKLAHOMA.*

*SEE THOR: GOD OF THUNDER #19-24. —WIL

RIGHT. I WAS THERE. I SAW WHAT HAPPENED TO BROXTON.

WHAT DOES SHE KNOW ABOUT BROXTON? WHO *IS* THIS LADY?

SHOULDN'T HAVE SAID THAT. THE ODINSON MAY HAVE TRUSTED THIS WOMAN, BUT HE DIDN'T HAVE A SECRET TO HIDE.

SO...YOU BELIEVE AGGER HAS BEEN KIDNAPPED BY HIS CORPORATE RIVALS?

GIVEN THE SCENE AT THE BANK, YEAH, THAT'S MY HUNCH.

AND YOU BELIEVE THEY MEAN *HARM* TO ROXXON, PERHAPS EVEN TO AGGER HIMSELF?

DOESN'T EVERYONE?

THEN I HAVE A VERY IMPORTANT QUESTION FOR YOU, AGENT SOLOMON...

WHY EXACTLY SHOULD WE ATTEMPT TO *STOP* THEM?

THAT *IS* AN IMPORTANT QUESTION.

AND IF THERE WASN'T AN EQUALLY IMPORTANT ANSWER, BELIEVE ME, I'D BE READY TO KNOCK OFF EARLY AND SIP SOME MAI TAIS BY THE POOL.

BUT I'M AFRAID THERE *IS* SUCH AN ANSWER...

"...IT'S CALLED THE *AGGER IMPERATIVE*. AND IT'S SOMETHING WE HAVE TO AVOID AT ALL COSTS."

MEANWHILE. NOT FAR AWAY.

WARNING. THIS FACILITY IS UNDER ATTACK.

THREAT LEVEL OMEGA. LETHAL FORCE IS AUTHORIZED AND ENCOURAGED.

DOOMSDAY SCENARIO IS IN EFFECT! STATUS UPDATE, PEOPLE!

SATELLITE UPLOAD AT 79 PERCENT. ALL SERVERS ARE SET TO FRY BEFORE BEING ACCESSED.

STILL TRIANGULATING THE NANITE TRACKING AGENT IN MR. AGGER'S BLOOD. SHOULD HAVE A G.P.S. LOCK ANY SECOND NOW.

READY TO DEPLOY THE *BERSERKER SQUAD*.

THE 'ZERKERS?! HAVE THEY EVEN BEEN FIELD-TESTED YET?

WE DON'T HAVE TIME FOR FIELD TESTING! THIS IS NOT A DRILL, FOLKS! WE ARE COUNTING DOWN UNTIL THE AGGER IMPERATIVE KICKS IN, AND WE ALL KNOW WHAT *THAT--*

WE HAVE MULTIPLE UNITS DOWN AND TARGET INCOMING! ANYONE NOT CHAINED TO A TERMINAL, STAND UP AND FALL IN, NOW!

BUT... I WENT TO M.I.T.

THEN YOU'RE SMART ENOUGH TO USE THIS. LET'S GO.

WAIT, I'M JUST A TECH! PLEASE DON'T KILL ME, MR. HARADA!

I...I WROTE A PAPER ON YOU IN COLLEGE. I GOT A B+.

THEN I SUPPOSE YOU CAN GUESS WHAT THIS IS.

OH, GOD.

THIS IS HARADA. CONTROL ROOM DISABLED.

AGGER IMPERATIVE IS A GO. WILL RENDEZVOUS IN--

BOOM

KLANG

UGGH--!

--WE'RE HERE TO SERVE A LAWFUL *SEARCH WARRANT.*

WE'RE HERE AS AGENTS OF *S.H.I.E.L.D.*

FROM EARTH.

MIDGARD.

WHATEVER. WE'RE HERE TO SEARCH THE QUARTERS OF *JANE FOSTER.*

WITH YOUR ROYAL PERMISSION, OF COURSE.

OR WITHOUT.

I MUST SAY, MY FIRST INCLINATION IS TO HAVE YOUR HEADS FORCIBLY REMOVED FROM YOUR SHOULDERS AND CATAPULTED BACK TO MIDGARD.

BUT JANE FOSTER AND HER *CONGRESS OF WORLDS* HAVE PROVEN THEMSELVES TO BE A SOURCE OF SOME ANNOYANCE TO THIS COURT.

JUST YESTERMORN, THEY DARED DEMAND THAT ONE OF MY *THUNDER GUARD* BE STRIPPED OF HIS HAMMER, BECAUSE THEY SAY HE BRUTALIZES TROLLS *"WITHOUT CAUSE."*

THE *CAUSE* IS THAT THEY'RE *TROLLS!*

IF THERE'S A CHANCE THIS INVESTIGATION OF YOURS COULD LEAVE ME WITH ONE LESS SENATOR-SIZED THORN IN MY SIDE, THEN BY ALL MEANS, ALLOW MY GUARDS TO SHOW YOU TO JANE FOSTER'S QUARTERS.

AND PERHAPS SOMEONE SHOULD ROUND UP THE GOOD CONGRESSWOMAN HERSELF.

OH, THAT WON'T BE NECESSARY, MR. CUL.

OR LIKELY EVEN POSSIBLE. SOMETHING TELLS ME THAT MS. FOSTER...

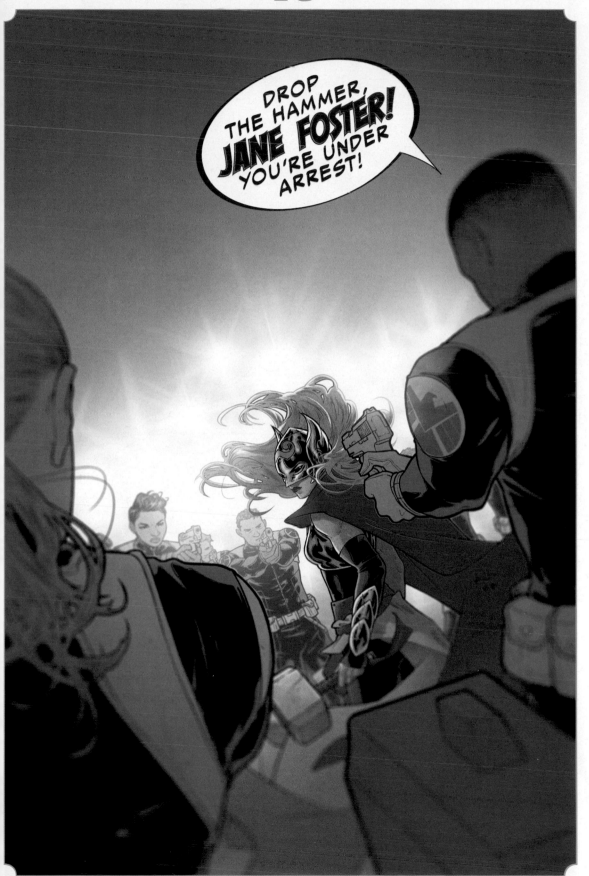

10

THE BATTLE OF ROXXON ISLAND

MIDGARD.
ROXXON ISLAND.
SOMEWHERE IN
THE SKIES ABOVE
MANHATTAN.

CONGRATULATIONS.
AS OF FIVE MINUTES
AGO, YOU ALL RECEIVED
A *RAISE*. NOW ALL
YOU HAVE TO DO...

...IS *SURVIVE*
LONG ENOUGH
TO EARN IT.

WELCOME
TO ACTIVE DUTY,
MEN AND WOMEN
OF *STRIKEFORCE
B.E.R.S.E.R.K.E.R.*

APPARENTLY
THESE PEOPLE ARE
WORKING UNDER THE
MISCONCEPTION THAT
THEY CAN SPIT IN
OUR FACES AND GET
AWAY WITH IT.

BUT WE ARE NOT
ALCHEMAX, LADIES
AND GENTLEMEN. WE ARE
NOT THOSE WEAK-KNEED
PENCIL-PUSHERS OVER
AT OSCORP OR STANE
INTERNATIONAL.

WE ARE
ROX-@#%*-
XON.

AND IF GOD
ALMIGHTY EVER
DARED SPIT IN OUR
DIRECTION, THERE'D
BE BLOOD IN
HEAVEN BY THE
SABBATH.

SO YOU'RE
GONNA GO *FIND*
THE MAN WHO SIGNS
OUR PAYCHECKS AND
BRING HIM BACK WHERE
HE BELONGS. YOU WILL
SCOUR THE DAMN
EARTH IF YOU
HAVE TO.

YOUR BACKUP HAS ALREADY ARRIVED.

IT'S ABOUT TIME! THOR NEEDS HELP IN THE MAIN HALLWAY AND MIDAS HAS ME PINNED DOWN IN THE--

RIGHT. WHERE DID YOU SAY THOR WAS AGAIN?

RRRRRGGHH!!!

TWO HUNDRED THIRTY-NINE.

THAT'S HOW MANY *TEXTS* WE FOUND ON THIS PHONE.

ALSO KNOWN AS *CAPTAIN AMERICA.*

TEXTS BETWEEN *YOU* AND A CERTAIN *SAM WILSON.*

SOME OF THE TEXTS WERE EVEN OF A RATHER...

LET'S SAY, *UNSEEMLY* NATURE.

QUITE UNSEEMLY.

THOR DOES NOT HAVE A PHONE. OR TIME TO WASTE.

SHE DOESN'T, HUH?

RIGHT, MAYBE SHE DOESN'T.

BUT *JANE FOSTER* SURE DOES.

IT'S HER PHONE. WE TOOK IT FROM HER ROOM ON ASGARDIA.

SOME TECHS FROM ROXXON WERE MORE THAN HAPPY TO HELP US HACK INTO IT.

SO THOR, WHY DO YOU THINK JANE FOSTER IS GETTING TEXTS FROM CAPTAIN AMERICA?

WHY DO YOU THINK SHE'S LYING ABOUT HAVING CANCER?

LYING?!

WHY DON'T YOU TAKE OFF THE HELMET AND TELL US ALL ABOUT IT.

TAKE OFF THE HELMET, JANE FOSTER.

AND DROP THE HAMMER.

YOU'RE COMING WITH US.

YOU'RE GONNA ANSWER OUR QUESTIONS WHETHER YOU LIKE IT OR NOT.

MIGHTY THOR # 8 VARIANT
BY **GREG HILDEBRANDT**

11

THOR'S BEST FRIEND

OUR INVESTIGATION, ALL THE EVIDENCE...

...EVERYTHING POINTED TO...

HOW... HOW IS THIS...

NO TIME. CAN'T HOLD THIS FOR LONG.

YOU'RE A DOCTOR. YOU KNOW HOW TO SAVE YOU. THINK IT AND I'LL KNOW TOO.

JUST HURRY.

SO...WE WERE WRONG. BUT WE'VE *NEVER* BEEN WRONG.

IT DOESN'T MATTER. EVERYONE'S STILL UNDER ARREST.

UP AGAINST THE WALL! ALL OF--

"ROXXON ISLAND... IS TURNING TO GOLD."

THOR, COME IN!

I STILL CAN'T BELIEVE WE WERE WRONG. I WAS SO SURE IT WAS HER.

IT MADE A LOT OF SENSE. THOUGH WHEN I LOOK AT HER NOW...

RIGHT. HOW COULD WE HAVE BEEN SO STUPID?

A PUNY LITTLE THING LIKE THAT.

DON'T THEY, DARIO?

I'VE NEVER HEARD OF ANY "AGGER IMPERATIVE."

THE ENGINES MUST'VE BEEN KNOCKED OUT WHEN ROXXON ISLAND WAS RUTHLESSLY ATTACKED BY MIDAS AND HARADA. I'M THE REAL VICTIM HERE.

RIGHT. TELL IT TO THE JUDGE.

I DON'T HAVE TO.

THAT'S WHAT *THEY'RE* FOR...

WE'RE THE *ROXXON LEGAL TEAM.* WE'LL NEED A LIST OF EVERYONE'S NAMES. WE'RE *SUING* YOU ALL.

WE'RE *ALSO* SUING THE MIDAS FOUNDATION AND YASHIDA INDUSTRIES. AND THE MAKERS OF THE ENGINES ON ROXXON ISLAND.

ER, IT WAS A ROXXON SUBSIDIARY WHO MADE THE ENGINES.

WE'LL SELL THE COMPANY, *THEN* SUE IT.

HEH. I'VE GOT *WAY* MORE LAWYERS THAN YOU, AGGER. AND MINE ARE *NINJAS.*

I'VE BEEN TO JAIL BEFORE. DOESN'T TEND TO STICK. AND AFTER TODAY, I'LL STILL BE RICHER THAN YOU WHEN I GET OUT, DARIO.

IF YOU GET OUT.

I'LL MAKE SURE THE SHANK THAT KILLS YOU IS DIPPED IN GOLD.

I'LL HELP YOU FILE A FORMAL COMPLAINT WHENEVER YOU'RE READY, DR. FOSTER.

JANE.

I BELIEVE SHE ONCE TOLD YOU TO CALL HER JANE.

YES, I DID. BUT...PERHAPS IT *IS* TIME FOR ME TO GET BACK TO ASGARDIA.

I CAN FEEL MY...CANCER BECOMING... *IRRITABLE*.

YEAH, OF COURSE, JANE, IN YOUR CONDITION, YOU'VE GOT TO...

NO. NOT YET.

THOR, WHAT ARE YOU...

I WANT HER TO KNOW THE TRUTH.

I WOULDN'T MIND KNOWING SOME MYSELF.

VERY WELL.

IT TOOK A TREMENDOUS AMOUNT OF POWER TO MAKE TODAY HAPPEN. I DON'T KNOW THAT WE COULD DO IT AGAIN. NOT WITHOUT A CENTURY OR SO OF REST.

IF THIS IS HOW YOU WISH THE DAY TO END, THEN SO BE IT, THOR. TRUTH BE TOLD...I WOULD EXPECT NO LESS OF YOU.

YOUR HEART IS STRONGER THAN EVEN YOUR THUNDER, MY LADY.

THAT'S WHAT MAKES YOU WORTHY.

THAT'S WHY I CHOSE YOU.

MIGHTY THOR # 11 VARIANT
BY **PASQUAL FERRY** & **FRANK D'ARMATA**

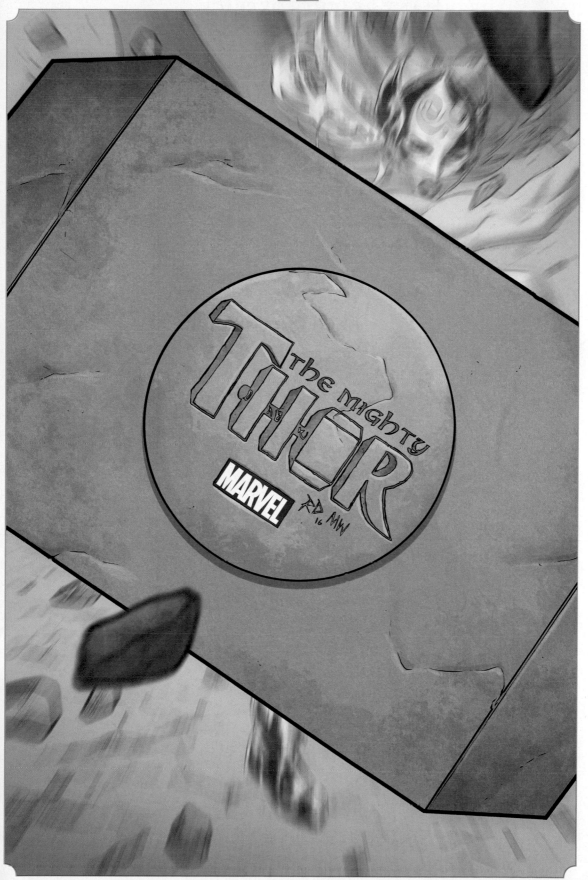

12

THE UNTOLD ORIGIN OF MJOLNIR

THE DISTANT REACHES OF SPACE.

...WITH BLOODSHED AND WAR.

A YOUNG WARLORD NAMED ULIK HAD UNITED THE CLANS OF ROCK TROLLS AND INVADED NIDAVELLIR, THE REALM OF THE DWARVES.

BATTLE RAGED THROUGHOUT THE SKORNHEIM MOUNTAINS.

UNTIL ALL-FATHER ODIN ARRIVED, LEADING THE ARMIES OF ASGARD.

IT WASN'T THAT THE ALL-FATHER HELD ANY GREAT LOVE FOR DWARVES. THOUGH HE DID HAVE TREMENDOUS AFFECTION FOR THE KILLING OF TROLLS.

ODIN MADE WAR BECAUSE HE KNEW THE DWARVES' MINES AND FORGES WERE OF VITAL IMPORTANCE TO ALL THE TEN REALMS.

THE BATTLE WAS SWIFT AND BRUTAL.

AND QUITE DECISIVE.

THE TROLLS HAVE RETREATED BACK INTO THEIR SLOP HOLES, LORD ODIN. NIDAVELLIR BELONGS ONCE MORE TO THE SONS OF IVALDI.

THEN FEEL FREE TO RETURN THERE, MASTER DWARF.

NOT WITHOUT FIRST BESTOWING ON YOU A *GIFT*, YOUR MAGNIFICENCE. A TOKEN OF OUR APPRECIATION.

AND A SYMBOL OF THE UNBREAKABLE BOND THAT HAS BEEN BUILT BETWEEN THE DWARVES AND THE GODS.

IT WAS A NUGGET OF *RAW URU*. THE RAREST, MOST MYSTICAL METAL IN ALL THE REALMS.

MINED FROM DEEP BENEATH THE MOUNTAINS OF NIDAVELLIR. VIRTUALLY UNBREAKABLE, IT WAS SAID.

UNSMELTABLE, EVEN. SO STRONG NOT EVEN THE FURNACES OF THE DWARVES COULD MELT IT.

ODIN GREETED THE GIFT WITH THE EXPECTED COURTESY.

A ROCK. I SAVE THEIR TINY SCRAGGLY-BEARDED LIVES AND THEY BRING ME A *ROCK*.

SUCH A *FITTING GIFT*, SONS OF NIDAVELLIR. WHENEVER I LOOK UPON THIS...

...SMALL AND UTTERLY USELESS THING...

...I WILL BE REMINDED OF *DWARVES*.

SOME SAID URU WAS A VESTIGE OF THE EARLIEST OF DAYS. RUBBLE FROM THE ROCK OF CREATION ITSELF.

VERY FEW THINGS HAVE EVER ENDURED THAT LONG.

THE STORM WAS ONE OF THEM.

IT BEGAN WITH THE FIRST WIND THAT EVER HOWLED DOWN OUT OF THE VOID, AND IT HAD BEEN GROWING IN SIZE AND FURY WITH EACH SUBSEQUENT EON.

THEY CALLED IT THE GOD TEMPEST. THE MOTHER OF THUNDER.

YOU ALWAYS KNEW IT WAS COMING WHEN EVEN THE SPACE SHARKS FLED IN TERROR. BUT BY THEN, IT WAS ALREADY TOO LATE.

ITS WINDS BLEW COMETS OFF COURSE, RIPPED WORLDS FROM THEIR ORBIT, AND SNUFFED OUT STARS LIKE FLICKERING CANDLES.

ITS LIGHTNING LEFT CLOUDS OF DUST WHERE ONCE WERE MOONS. ITS THUNDER MADE EVEN BLACK HOLES TREMBLE.

IT WAS A COSMIC THUNDERSTORM THE SIZE OF A GALAXY, ONE THAT HAD BEEN RAGING SINCE THE BEGINNING OF TIME. BUT IT WAS MORE THAN THAT AS WELL.

THE WORST OF ITS WRATH WAS RESERVED ONLY FOR THOSE WHO TRULY DESERVED IT, IT WAS SAID. A STORM THAT PASSED JUDGMENT. ALMOST AS IF...

...AS IF IT HAD A MIND OF ITS OWN.

A SENTIENT SUPER STORM.

AND ONE DAY, AS IT HAPPENED, THAT STORM'S JUDGMENT...

...CAME EVEN FOR THE GODS.

THE GODS OF ASGARD HAD FACED TROLLS AND DRAGONS AND DEMONS OF FIRE AND ALL MANNER OF GIANTS.

BUT THEY HAD NEVER FOUGHT A STORM.

HOW DOES ONE KILL A HURRICANE THAT CONSUMES PLANETS? TO BEGIN WITH...

...IT HELPS TO BE THE ALL-FATHER.

YOU CALL THIS A STORM?! ODIN *BATHES* IN FIERCER MAELSTROMS! ODIN'S *SNORES* ARE LOUDER THAN THIS MEDIOCRE THUNDER!

COME, LITTLE GALE, THE ALL-FATHER OF ASGARD WILL SHOW YOU THE FURY OF A *THOUSAND* STORMS!

THEY BATTLED FOR MANY DAYS.

THE GOD TEMPEST AND THE GOD OF GODS.

HAIL FELL LIKE A BLIZZARD OF DAGGERS. ODIN'S SPEAR PIERCED THE SKY AND HIS ROARS CRACKED THE RAINBOW BRIDGE. RAIN GUSHED LIKE BLOOD.

BUT STILL THERE WAS NO END TO THE WINDS.

OR TO THE MIND-STAGGERING POWER OF THE ODIN-FORCE.

YET EVEN THE MIGHTIEST OF STORMS MUST EVENTUALLY GROW TIRED. AND WHEN THE ALL-FATHER COULD SENSE HIS OPPONENT WEAKENING...

...HE STRUCK WITH ALL HIS ALMIGHTY MIGHT.

LORD ODIN?

IT IS...

...DONE...

THE ALL-FATHER HAD *TRAPPED* THE STORM *INSIDE* THE URU. THROUGH WHAT DARK AND PRIMAL MAGIC, EVEN HE COULD NOT SAY.

THOUGH HE KNEW EXACTLY WHAT TO DO NEXT.

THE DWARVES STOKED THEIR FIRES FOR THREE DAYS, UNTIL THEIR CAVES AND MOUNTAINS WERE MELTING AROUND THEM.

BUT STILL THEY COULD NOT SMELT THE URU.

SO THEY HOOKED A STAR AND DRAGGED IT INTO THEIR FURNACES.

BY THE MORROW, THE STAR WAS DEAD, THE MOUNTAINTOPS WERE OOZING LAVA, AND THE SOUNDS OF FORGING RANG OUT ACROSS THE REALMS.

HEAVE!

NO ONE IS SURE HOW MANY DWARVES IT TOOK TO POUND THE METAL INTO SHAPE. SOME SAY DOZENS. OTHERS SAY HUNDREDS. BOTH ESTIMATES ARE LIKELY CONSERVATIVE.

THOSE DWARVES WHO CLAIMED TO HAVE BEEN THERE WOULD LATER SPEAK IN AWE...OF HOW THE METAL FOUGHT THEM 'TIL THE BITTER END. AS IF THE GOD TEMPEST WAS STILL RAGING INSIDE THE URU.

FOR 17 DAYS, THE CLANGING RANG LIKE THUNDER. UNTIL EVERY TOOL IN NIDAVELLIR WAS SHATTERED AND EVERY DWARF EXHAUSTED. UNTIL THE SKORNHEIM MOUNTAINS THEMSELVES BEGAN TO CRUMBLE.

BUT THE DWARVES ARE THE FINEST BLACKSMITHS IN ALL THE REALMS, AND ONCE THEY WERE FINISHED, ALL WOULD AGREE...

...THEY HAD FORGED THEIR FINEST CREATION.

THEY DELIVERED THE WEAPON TO ODIN, AS PROMISED. THOUGH WITH ONE CAVEAT...

...THAT THEY WOULD NEVER HAVE TO SEE THAT DAMNED HAMMER AGAIN.

I NAME THEE...

...MJOLNIR, THE THUNDER WEAPON.

FIRST AMONG HAMMERS. THE BREAKER OF ALL THINGS.

COME, MJOLNIR. LET US SEE WHAT YOU CAN--

ODIN'S RIDE HAD NEARLY DESTROYED ASGARD. HE FORBADE ANYONE FROM EVER SPEAKING OF IT AGAIN.

THE WEAPON WAS TOO UNBRIDLED, HE SWORE. TOO WILD AND UNTAMED FOR EVEN THE GODS. AND IF IT WOULD NOT BE WIELDED BY HIM, THEN IT COULD ROT, FOR ALL HE CARED.

SO THE ALL-FATHER PLACED ENCHANTMENTS ON THE HAMMER THAT WOULD MAKE IT ALL BUT IMPOSSIBLE FOR ANYONE ELSE TO EVER LIFT IT.

AND THEN MJOLNIR WAS LEFT TO GATHER DUST IN THE WEAPONS HALL OF ASGARD.

AND THERE IT SAT FOR MANY EONS.

FORGOTTEN.

WAITING.

POOR GIRL. STILL SO FOOLISH AND BLIND.

ALL TALES ABOUT GODS BEGIN THE SAME. AND I'M AFRAID THEY END THE SAME AS WELL.

"IN DEATH.

"DEATH AND DESTRUCTION."

AND. WAR.

SO MUCH WAR...

THE WAR OF THE REALMS

THE BOOK OF THE MADGOG

THE BATTLE OF HONEY BROOK

TO BE CONTINUED.

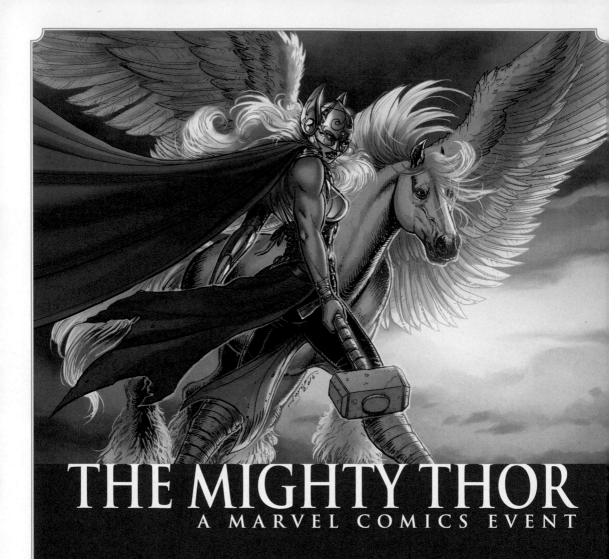

THE MIGHTY THOR
A MARVEL COMICS EVENT

CIVIL
WAR

MIGHTY THOR # 6 CIVIL WAR VARIANT
BY **JOYCE CHIN** & **LAURA MARTIN**

MIGHTY THOR # 8 STORY THUS FAR VARIANT
BY **MARGUERITE SAUVAGE**

MIGHTY THOR # 10 MARVEL TSUM TSUM TAKEOVER VARIANT
BY **NATACHA BUSTOS**

- paisley head scarf

- some scarves as previous look

- loose-fitting shirt b/c of weight loss

- braided leather belt, different from outfit 2

- chinos, not denim

- bald, no eyebrows, no makeup
- very pale

- canvas shoes w/ rubber sole, from different outfit 2

Height

hazel eyes

skin

white piping

ginger/
orangey-red
hair

- lips painted
on to mask,
"lipstick
kiss" look

poncho/cape
w/ arm slits

- gold gun,
rivets, &
garter rings

red
half-wedge
heels w/
2 spike
blades

holster

war paint splattered on tips of horns

textured cloak, mottled browns & warm greens

- wispy/patchy facial hair braided into 3 small chin braids

- Bigger, more muscular than regular Loki (but not as bulky as the Odinson)

- chest tattoo based on Norse symbol:

- snake coils down arms

FREE
DIGITAL COPY